Praise for *Wonderland*

"My first thought about the poems in Matthew Dickman's new collection, *Wonderland*, was: *Why doesn't every poet write this way?* . . . I wish others wrote with Dickman's clarity and ability to engage. . . . These poems light both heart and mind. They stab you with memory's shiny knife. 'Ouch,' you say, and then 'thank you.' " —David Kirby, *New York Times*

"Tender and troubling, dark and glowing. . . . [F]ull of glimpses of sudden violence and hidden traumas, which often simultaneously mix with tenderness, love and indeed a certain sense of wonder." —Brandon Yu, *San Francisco Chronicle*

"[Dickman's] ability not only to recollect but also to relive his childhood in the present moment, as if boy and man coexisted and conversed with each other, manifests a hard-won wisdom." —*Library Journal*

"The poems are ferocious and hardened by a backdrop of addiction and poverty. . . . In Dickman's poems, readers observe as the bright-eyed potential of youth is shattered by the devastation of adulthood's onset." —*Publishers Weekly*

"[Dickman's] imagination, the possibility of better, helped him filter and preserve from the sharp and rusty clutter the beautiful moments of childhood. Thus, the collection relates a sweetness it should by all accounts be unable to render."   —Brian Juenemann, *Register-Guard*

"Dickman reenters youth in all its peaks and valleys—without exaggeration or cliché. . . . While many of Dickman's poems tell stories and carry narratives across poems, they also follow their own meandering logic, like a late night conversation."   —Emma Winters, *America: The Jesuit Review*

"There is an unabashed rapture to these poems about ordinary American life in the analog age. How astounding, and how perfectly troubling, to be led through this fearsome, familiar realm of choked silences and violent collisions by an intelligence as deft and buoyant as Matthew Dickman's."

—Tracy K. Smith, United States poet laureate

"A wonderful new poetic voice writing warm and cozy visions of old Portland, Oregon. I loved it."—Gus Van Sant, Academy Award–nominated filmmaker

"With *Wonderland*, Matthew Dickman captures the vicissitudes of childhood: the mess and wildness of it all, how we are both held and discarded, the way darkness subsumes the glow and vice versa. Dickman's poems are deft and sparkling and never cease to tear into you with their profound rawness and beauty."

—Carrie Brownstein, star of *Portlandia* and author of
Hunger Makes Me a Modern Girl

WONDERLAND

WONDERLAND

POEMS

MATTHEW DICKMAN

W. W. NORTON & COMPANY

Independent Publishers Since 1923

The lines from "Terza Rima". Copyright © 2016 by the Adrienne Rich Literary Trust.
Copyright © 2001 by Adrienne Rich, from *Collected Poems: 1950–2012* by Adrienne Rich.
Used by permission of W. W. Norton & Company, Inc.

For information about permission to reproduce selections from this book, write to
Permissions, W. W. Norton & Company, Inc., 500 Fifth Avenue, New York, NY 10110

For information about special discounts for bulk purchases, please contact
W. W. Norton Special Sales at specialsales@wwnorton.com or 800-233-4830

Manufacturing by LSC Communications, Harrisonburg
Book design by JAM Design
Production manager: Beth Steidle

Library of Congress Cataloging-in-Publication Data

Names: Dickman, Matthew, author.
Title: Wonderland : poems / Matthew Dickman.
Description: First edition. | New York : W. W. Norton & Company, 2018
Identifiers: LCCN 2017052697 | ISBN 9780393634068 (hardcover)
Classification: LCC PS3604.I2988 A6 2018 | DDC 811/.6—dc23
LC record available at https://lccn.loc.gov/2017052697

ISBN 978-0-393-35790-5 pbk.

W. W. Norton & Company, Inc., 500 Fifth Avenue, New York, N.Y. 10110
www.wwnorton.com

W. W. Norton & Company Ltd., 15 Carlisle Street, London W1D 3BS

1 2 3 4 5 6 7 8 9 0

FOR JULIA, HAMZA, AND OWEN

IN MEMORY OF C. K. WILLIAMS

There are so many roots to the tree of anger

—AUDRE LORDE

It's tough, kid, but it's life

—DEAD KENNEDYS

I hate hate

—REAGAN YOUTH

Was that youth?   that clear

sapphire on snow

—ADRIENNE RICH

CONTENTS

WONDERLAND

TEENAGE RIOT

All of us were boys only some were taller or already in high school, and almost
    nothing else
mattered but to learn some new trick,
to pull off something we saw in a skate video, wind cutting
around our bodies when we flew
off the lip of a ramp, grabbed the board and twisted
into a 180, kicking
a leg out and landing it, the only way to run
through the neighborhood

was to run through it
together, flipping off cops and skinheads, I almost
don't even remember girls but a vague sense of the taste of bubble gum
and how they smelled so different
from us, sitting in some kid's basement drinking
his parents' vodka, we grew out our bangs, moved in a pack,
jumped in when some one of us
got jumped,

so when a man we had never seen before
came up and started beating on Simon, one of us dropped his skateboard, walked
over to the man
like someone walking into a bank

and stabbed him.

The man, startled, sat down, right there on the asphalt,

right in the middle of his new consciousness,

kind of looking around.

TRANSUBSTANTIATION

My mother is taking

me to the store

because it's hot out and I'm sick and want a Popsicle. All the other kids

are at school sitting

in rows of small desks, looking

out the window.

She is wearing one of those pantsuits

with shoulder pads

and carrying a purse with a checkbook. We are holding hands, standing in

front of the big automatic doors

which silently swing open

so we can

walk in together, so we can

step out of the heat and step

into a world of fluorescent light and cool, cool air.

Then, as if a part of the heat

had suddenly broken off,

had become its own power, a man

places his arm around her

shoulders but also around her neck

and she lets go of my hand and pushes me

away. Pushes me toward

the safety of the checkout line. Then the man begins to yell.

And then the man begins to cry.

The pyramid

of canned beans in front of me

is so perfect

I can't imagine anyone needing beans

bad enough

to destroy it. The man is walking my mother

down one aisle and then another aisle

and then another

like a father dragging

his daughter toward a wedding he cannot find.

Everyone is

standing so still. All you can hear

is my mom pleading

and the sound of the air conditioner like *Shhhhhhhhh*.

THE ORDER OF THINGS

Now when I think of the second grade I think about fall leaves,

black oaks, and urine.

I think about being caught in the bathroom, swinging

from the bar above the door to the whitewashed stall and how I was

dragged out by my arm

and how it felt like my arm was an avocado

someone had stabbed with a knife

to remove the pit,

and how I was

made to stand before each of my teachers and tell them

I couldn't go to the bathroom by myself, *Tell them*

you don't know

how—said God's adult, the nun

who found me, who now leads me

to each classroom,

like following the Stations of the Cross.

And at each station—

the girl who'd been forced

to stand the whole day

over the spot where she peed

in the library, the kid who was made to wear a piece

of pink string

around his wrist,

a reminder

not to pee in his pants,

the boy who was marched through the mall, past the food court and arcade,

pushed along

by his father

who had made a sign,

made it from scratch, a sign

the boy was wearing around his neck, that read *I wet the bed*, and how

no one tried to stop it.

ONE A.M.

I went outside to see if I was there.
I went around the corner of the first time we met.
I went into your bedroom and found a little bit of night but just enough.
I went and got sick and now I don't know what to do.
I went to school and was punished.
I went to school and sat in the coatroom and was on fire.
I went outside and the sky was a computer program with no father.
I went home early.
I went to the store and thought of Allen.
I went over my happiness to see if I could see you.
I went into the citrus coffee cups of your hands and stayed there.
I went to my mother and asked her to shut up.
I went to my mother and asked if she would hold me.
I went into a city I didn't know and I was OK with it.
I went into a city I didn't know and something like an accident killed me.
I went home after the car accident and you sat beside me.
I went over to your house and destroyed things.
I went but I didn't know what I was doing.
I went behind the garbage can to be OK.
I went on vacation and lived like a boat for three days.
I went for it.
I went into the forest and all my friends were digging up their brains.
I went to sea and thought this is what I came for.
I went into the city of hammers and rang like a bell and rang like a bell.

WHITE POWER

They took an Ethiopian soccer player

and split his head open with a baseball bat. Trees

were standing around, cars were driving by.

My mother was making chipped beef and toast.

We never borrowed milk from the neighbors

though sometimes we had no money

for milk. My sister thought any man taller than me

was her father.

ASTRONAUT

What does it

what does it

what does it

feel like to walk in space, to walk on the moon, and then come back,

come home and cook your dinner inside a microwave oven?

Is it like when Michael was fourteen and walked into the Checkers Mart

on 92nd Avenue with a gun under his white T-shirt? His long legs

spacewalking between the aisles, all the different

colors of candy and car oil, moving through

the gravity like ice water. Is it like that? And what about

the cashier behind the counter? Standing there, Mission Control

watching him like coordinates on a screen, like you

would watch anything you thought you knew, but you don't know,

you don't know

you don't know

you don't know.

WONDERLAND

Caleb is standing in his front yard
hitting a stick

against a tree. In three months he will
be in the fifth grade.

He's thinking
about He-Man and She-Ra,

about Castle Grayskull.
Inside the house

his dad is screaming at his mom.
Now Caleb's throwing the stick

in the air
and imagining it's a sword on fire

that only he can catch.
When his dad leaves

Caleb will go into the house
and find his mom in the weird dark

of his parents' bedroom
where he will kiss her busted lip, crawl

onto the bed and hold her,
his arms just beneath

her ribs. Eventually
he will go back

out into the yard,
pick up the once flaming sword, and wait.

TWO A.M.

I lost my body in the fight for my body.
I lost my brother because his body hated him so much.
I lost time.
I lost the way and was happy and the moon was above me.
I lost the feeling in my fingers.
I lost some friends but found a secret room in my apartment.
I lost the chandelier light behind your shoulder blade.
I lost 1975.
I lost the hat you gave me and have never been the same.
I lost the polar bears and I lost the tigers and I lost the elephants.
I lost the ship at sea.
I lost the bottle.
I lost the rib that God gave and the rib that God took away.
I lost the sheet you had cut the two holes in for my eyes to see through.
I lost all my money.
I lost nothing that might have kept me alive.
I lost the light in the puddle with my face in it and a stick.
I lost the way to be with you.
I lost the wind coming through my window and the bed below it.
I lost blood.
I lost blood and stars and the fifth grade.
I lost paint-by-numbers and the color yellow and blue make.
I lost all my fillings.
I lost a fight in which I paid cash to fall and not get up and never get up.

STRAWBERRY MOON

It felt like the whole world
exhaled really fast like being
punched in the stomach.
Every song was about you.
I'm not kidding. Just
like in really bad songs and now
I can't listen to anything
because I'm like a fuzzy bumblebee
bouncing off all these stamens,
flicking them with my wet
chin and pretending
it's your stomach, honey, honey,
it feels like I'm never going
to be OK and summer
is coming no matter what.
Summer looks at me,
shakes its head
and says fuck you,
you should have prepared
for this, you should have been
a father but now you're like
a can of dog food and only
the dogs are excited
but you and I know that's only

because they don't know better,

that's only because they're pets

and have been beaten

with the daily paper they are

trained to bring inside

and lay at the big hairless feet

of their masters. Lay. Lie.

I only ever wanted you to tell me

to sit. And now more than ever

I'm going to die, and that's on me

I know, I know that's my deal,

that's my fault, that's what

they say, and they should.

I keep praying it's only summer

talking, that it's only the dogs

barking, I keep looking at houses

we could live in like someone

shot in the head and asking

the people screaming

around him if he has something

on his face, he just can't figure

it out, dumb beast, gone but not

really even knowing he's gone.

LINOLEUM

Ryan had pictures of his mom
he would show

his friends, all of us
lost in the maze of sixth grade, reaching up

into the air of girls, and his mom
in a cheetah bra, laid back on the plastic

covering of the couch, her arms
folded across her body,

her hands
covering her crotch, her mouth

in a smile
and her eyes, I suppose, looking

into the eyes
of a man she had met and liked, a man

she had taken home, or a friend had
taken it for her, or she made her son take the pictures.

Ryan had a small stack of them
which he kept in a sock with yellow stripes on it.

My favorite picture of Ryan's mother
was the one where she is kneeling down in the kitchen,

naked but covered by her long
hair, her knees

pressed into the linoleum, the same floor
where she would stand

in the morning,
mix her vodka with orange juice, a new day

appearing in the street like a van
with its windows

painted black. She was so beautiful
and sweet to us. I remember

she laughed a lot.
You and I both know what Ryan did

with the pictures when he was alone,
and it wasn't anything short of dying.

He had found something
he could hold

in his hand like an alchemist,
a way of turning his shame from base metal into gold.

A VERY GOOD DOG

I must have looked so handsome because she said you look so handsome

and I must have been eight years old

because she said   I can't believe you are already

eight years old

and it must have been

a dark and romantic Italian restaurant

because it was dark in there and full of men and women holding hands

across the beautiful tables feeding each other

pasta and bread

and drinking wine and kissing and my mother with her Black Russian and me

with my Shirley Temple

and before we even sat down in the candlelight we must have

sat in the car because we were sitting in the car

in the pocket of the driveway where she placed her hand on my knee

and patted it like you would if the knee was

a very good dog

and she must have smiled and said   are you excited for our date

because she smiled and said are you excited for our date

and then combed my hair

because my hair must have

needed to be combed, to be made right.

And we must have danced that night

because the restaurant had a dance floor full of other couples and she showed me

where my hands were supposed to go

and how to move my legs

and laughed

and beamed and said   I love you so much

which meant there would be no other world

but this world,

no other way, no

other forest

but this forest and all the trees on fire and all the animals running.

THREE A.M.

The light invented who I was supposed to be.
The light told me I was king.
The light bent down and whispered shame on you.
The light huddled around the house.
The light arrived and was the shape of a stamp.
The light pours and pours.
The light slipped around your finger like a ring.
The light lifted up the gown.
The light slipped into the pilot's left pupil and sang.
The light left.
The light did not care who I was though it knew I was bad.
The light was Atlantic.
The light crawled and begged across my bedroom floor.
The light did not shiver.
The light pooled when the blood pooled and your fingernails.
The lighthouse.
The lightroom.
The light bought drinks and loved the children in the park.
The light came down and taught everyone a lesson.
The light made a pillow and then went to bed and didn't get up.
The light you are standing in.
The light turned against me because it's the right thing to do.
The light on the table and the pencil.
The light was electric and glass and broke when I punched it.

DIRTY ROTTEN IMBECILES

The crows are crazy.
It's like they are the only things that love
each other here,
in the air
moving away from each other, clouds of death-smoke-empires,
then coming back, lighting and
alighting and lightning. It's good
to return. Black lightning and soft.
They see everything and let it
happen. They let the men happen to the women
and the women happen to the children,
they let the lilac trees blossom in the rain, the maples drop
their leaves. They let the Rottweilers sleep
in the grassless backyards. They let the cats get run over
and the moon rise.

ORCHARD

I liked the dream my brother's high school girlfriend kept having about
      the skinned and dead horses

hanging from willow trees, a whole, what do you call it?
      orchard of willow trees,

you would call it that, you would call it an orchard because of the fruit
      and the flies. I liked it because she wore

wool skirts that covered her knees and soft Easter egg-colored sweaters
      and she wore her hair,

which was always washed in some strawberry shampoo, in a bun
      and I like the dream

because in the winter she would wear a ski jacket to school and it dripped
      with ski-lift passes like medals,

they were like dry-cleaning stubs dry cleaners pin to the plastic bags
      over clothes, and so many of them

that she looked either very clean or highly decorated, a single white pearl
      in each of her white earlobes. Don't you

ever wonder about other people's ears? Ears that get pierced,
    that get a tongue pushing inside them,

ears that get pulled off, anyway it is true that people have had their ears
    pulled right off of them, and sometimes

that's an accident and sometimes it isn't. The sound must be awful,
    like a crowd of ants shoving through

the brains of some butter. The ears just falling through space like mice
    with bloody feet, really just like mice.

I like to sit at night on the back porch and listen to the neighbors and laugh
    when they laugh and cry when they cry.

FOR IAN SULLIVAN UPON JOINING
THE EASTSIDE WHITE PRIDE

Even now

Even now

Even now

no one can say that you were never a child. What our neighborhood

lacked in compassion it made up for in baseball   (stomp)

bats and chain-link fences. Asian mini-marts

and your parents' rage swelling inside your chest   (stomp)

like someone pumping up a basketball, like someone taking

a long drag off a cigarette.

Now when you get dressed you get dressed   (stomp)

for battle. People cross the street when they see you

like you were black. Like you weren't afraid of anything. Like there

was nothing you wouldn't do. But you are afraid   (stomp)

of everything

of everything

of everything.

FOUR A.M.

I made a way so nothing would ever work out.
I made cereal.
I made a crook in my arm for your face.
I made a star out of apple seeds and two of your hairpins.
I made a mess out of the party.
I made four plus four and then I made you cry.
I made my bed.
I made a bed that would be impossible to sleep on.
I made this thing happen.
I made my body get bad and then I made nothing.
I made a box with a horse on it for my mom when I was twelve.
I made a bee die.
I made a slug die with salt and it was forever.
I made dinner out of all the things I've been embarrassed about.
I made myself eat it.
I made no progress with Communion or cherry blossoms.
I made a sign of the cross and meant it.
I made snow out of my brain.
I made lost and found.
I made lost.
I made you think you were crazy and also laundry was hanging.
I made a place where I could go forever.
I made longing out of a toothbrush.
I made a goodbye and so long and fuck off and what are you doing.

BAD BRAINS

Walnuts gather around

the roots of the walnut tree, fall one at a time until there are many,

a hem of them,

a skirt of walnuts sweeping the ground.

Falling and then lifted back up into the branches

by crows, in the mouths of squirrels.

Some of the walnuts are rotten but most

of them are not.

Most of them are not bothering anyone.

Falling to earth,

swept into the schoolyard.

The walnuts wear brown snap-back

Starter caps

in between the blades of grass.

Someone across the street is stomping on them in steel-toed boots.

He's breaking their heads

open. All their heads.

Open up.

Then he's going to stomp the broken bits, the soft parts inside.

WONDERLAND

He must have woken up
in his bedroom

with a poster of the Sex Pistols
on one wall and *Star Wars*

on the other, two parts of him, Caleb
and the age he's supposed to be.

Socks and underwear all over
the floor and no

siblings on earth.
Later we are skating down Woodstock

past a yard with a small dog walking
up and down, we stop

and kick the fence
and then Caleb spits on the dog

who just barks so he spits on the dog
again, some of the phlegm

getting into the dog's eyes,
its long ears, Caleb keeps

spitting, begins to scream
at the dog, who is now overcome,

slamming its head into the fence,
and so Caleb does the same,

gets down on his hands and knees,
their two heads

crashing together sound like
a hammer coming down on a hand.

EIGHT A.M.

I happened to myself and everything disappeared.
I happened to be walking.
I happened and you were there and scared.
I happened to be an addict.
I happened with the glass in the bathtub.
I happened and there was a sound that came from heaven.
I happened and it was quiet.
I happened and your mouth blew open like a soda can.
I happened in high school.
I happened in my mother's lap and the dead starlings.
I happened to be standing next to you.
I happened to the room before the room hung itself.
I happened to be lying.
I happened to download all the things that make you insecure.
I happened and it began to rain.
I happened to be an orange you were eating.
I happened to be a body that moves like a long dash and hamburger.
I happened to be the stove door and the pretty lady, circa 1950.
I happened to be nothing important.
I happened like a cake full of lightbulbs and a bat.
I happened to be barefoot and a worm.
I happened to be the worm.
I happened to the scissors when they should happen to me.
I happened to be there when the dog turned back into a boy.

SACK OF RABBITS

There she is

There she is

There she is

my older sister, her tall body

reaching up, reaching out, toward anything.

That feels good.

Walking through downtown Los Angeles with her boyfriend and the heroin

he sold, brown packets of wasps.

I was born. She held me,

babysat, carried my twin brother and me through grocery aisles

like a mom in middle school. Her boyfriend

holding her hand, her heart like a sack of rabbits, skull-sized

motors in the dark. They are pulling half-smoked

cigarettes out of ashtrays. I love her for this.

I love her for getting clean and then getting drunk and back

and forth like

a tennis ball

a tennis ball

a tennis ball.

BAD LOVE

The light from the porch is like a floodlight, looking for bodies, my body
sitting next to my little sister's body, which is shaking because she is crying
because she

is heart

broken,

I want

my sister

to feel

whole again, I want her to be happy. We keep lifting beers to our mouths like
weightlifters lifting very small weights. I want her not to suffer but also I don't care.
I'm like

a mom

that way, the way

a mom is

happy

to have her

kids back in the house, no matter what, no matter the illness or shame, no matter
if they are back because they have failed, just happy

to take care

of them,

and hold

them, pretend

they are little

again, like me

with my sister, never wanting her to leave the porch, opening beer after beer

so she'll stay, never wanting her to stop being here, and because I am selfish

and afraid of

death, I'm fine

with her being

pulled apart

by grief, I'm fine

with the world

pulling her under, and I'm saying yeah I know, I'm so sorry, but really

I'm thinking let it be like this forever, let her cry and cry,

let her struggle

if it means

I get to hold

her, if it means

we never stop

drinking.

NINE A.M.

I don't know what happened.
I don't know what I look like and also this morning.
I don't get why with your feet and fingers.
I don't know where I will be buried.
I don't play any instrument and also October is coming.
I don't get the light's somatic response system.
I don't do this.
I don't do my brain in order of the Stations of the Cross.
I don't do fuck you give me some more.
I don't know how not to.
I don't know why I arrive without ever being somewhere.
I don't vanish and white sheets with two holes for eyes.
I don't steal flowers anymore.
I don't enter the cool-forest-dark and also it's a brain trust.
I don't do light everlasting.
I don't do a plastic bag around my head.
I don't campfire without you and your son and the beach grass.
I don't talk about the murder trial.
I don't not-ever-not talk about it because it's in everything.
I don't hashtag my heart.
I don't glass breaking at night.
I don't gas station at night.
I don't elevator between the floors of my brain.
I don't know what to do now that I've done all of this to you.

BLOOD MOON

I will not say I remember
because there is a death
in remembering, a ghost
beneath our bed, an empty
cage at the zoo, and I will
not say do you remember
because there is a killing
in that, a knife someone
is putting inside someone else,
a Glasbake mug of hemlock
I made 'cause I was thirsty.
I won't say it because it's not
true. I keep walking
around our apartment
like a guard looking
for your hairpins, I don't know
what I'm making out
of them, they seem so
beautiful to me and feel
like water in my hands,
water that never spills
onto the ground, when you
would cum all I wanted

were babies, babies everywhere.
I'm trying to manage my
dumb-dumb time machine
brain and be here. OK I'm here,
I'm here thinking about babies,
I'm standing here right now,
I know, I can feel it, some
gold leaf in you being licked
up by someone that doesn't
make you feel like dying.
Oh tulip, I remember
everything, every every every
thing, the light coming in
through the bamboo, walking
in the dark over the overpass
toward your place, and the black
silk pillow I hated, the picture
you posted of me back before time,
when I was still new, when I was
something you wanted too badly.

LOST BOYS

I am always doing this. Walking around the old neighborhood, always
sixteen, moody and stealing cigarettes.
Baby, even when we're fucking I'm back there with the dogs
and trash cresting

around the bus stop like a wave of what people can afford.
In the rain I'm wearing my brother's jeans, a book of matches in my pocket,
afraid of the people here, each match
tip melting into pink slime.

Even when you're swallowing me, honey, even when I'm standing
in our kitchen getting dinner started, or playing with your son
I'm there. I'm not getting beat up. I'm not high,
not really. I'm just walking around

looking up at a sky that looks like a closet, hating the birds
because it doesn't feel like they belong, just the sky and the street belong.
Just the rain and the boys
on the corner, boys who were born here, death tucked away

in their hands,

their bomber jackets, death in their teeth and ears, wind in their

pockets, when they smile

it's not like when you smile,

their faces stretch out like a police state, their shadows

covering the whole block.

NOON

I stayed inside while everyone else was with the others.
I stayed inside your body too long.
I stayed and I thought a country would rise from the water.
I stayed and stayed.
I stayed and addressed the crowd and it was no one.
I stayed in the darkest corner of your hair.
I stayed for the dishes and the towels.
I stayed inside the dotted I of my brain.
I stayed inside and waited for the Surgeon General to call my name.
I stayed near the light in your window and the red leaves.
I stayed long enough for your son to love me.
I stayed inside an unknown planet.
I stayed because I didn't know what else to do and also knives.
I stayed past my bedtime.
I stayed though I am a little boy with a bedtime and a mother-mind.
I stayed and helped clean up.
I stayed for the love of ferns and rain and the sand in your shoes.
I stayed and drew flowers on my arm.
I stayed and cut the flowers out.
I stayed because they told me there would be medicine.
I stayed because there was none.
I stayed for the sundial and the gas station and the Christmas lights.
I stayed though I was asked to leave.
I stayed because leaving is like a plane exploding inside a nursery.

WONDERLAND

Maybe children are always
in training for something.

Always being told to do something
they do not want to do.

Caleb and Michael and I
in jeans and T-shirts and long bangs.

You have to work hard for things
you want

is what parents say,
is what the wind says. The three of us

are skating near the Safeway
and Caleb jumps

off his skateboard,
walks across the street, walks right up

to this other kid and starts
beating him. All hands and legs.

Then he stops. Something stops
inside him. He comes back,

a father
breathing hard, his face like a door slammed shut,

and crosses the street,
returns to us,

some good news
with blood on his shirt,

Attila the Hun smiling, skating
home toward the seventh grade.

MINOR THREAT

A maple

in the middle of all of this, in the middle of what is struck

and who is doing the striking,

in the middle of stitches

and skateboards, of cement and tar and bark dust,

the quiet of its green leaves

greening out in the middle of the neighborhood, peed on by dogs

with jaws like cardboard boxes,

with owners like box cutters

drinking malt liquor, drinking RC Cola,

its leaves making the wind into a body that flies down the street

and scatters in the rusting front yards,

the roots

under us all, moving like medicine in the woody

dirt. The branches in any weather

are stronger than all the kids who swing from them,

who hang from them,

in the queasy Southeast Portland light.

MINIMUM WAGE

My mother and I are on the front porch lighting each other's cigarettes

as if we were on a ten-minute break from our jobs

at being a mother and son, just ten minutes

to steal a moment of freedom before clocking back in, before

putting the aprons back on, the paper hats,

washing our hands twice and then standing

behind the counter again,

hoping for tips, hoping the customers

will be nice, will say some kind word, the cool

front yard before us and the dogs

in the backyard shitting on everything.

We are hunched over, two extras on the set of *The Night of the Hunter*.

I am pulling a second cigarette out of the pack, a swimmer

rising from a pool of other swimmers. Soon we will go back

inside and sit in the yellow kitchen and drink

the rest of the coffee

and what is coming to kill us will pour milk

into mine and sugar into hers.

THREE P.M.

This room of my disappearing act and valentine.
This chest that's blown out and honey it's really OK.
This record player.
This bed and all the times it's been made and also drowning.
This sea and foam.
This time I have really gone and done it.
This time of buttons and pencils and surgical masks and seaweed.
This amphibian inner-organ green.
This smoke.
This pillowcase and razors and salt trying to be a human being.
This car alarm trying to be a human being.
This way of thinking and also climbing the stairs to who-knows-what.
This answer.
This couch and cutting board and carrots and lamplight.
This Mojave Desert.
This chrysalis branch that keeps breaking over my shoulders.
This kind of thing.
This going backwards so now I'm like a door in a house you knew.
This cellphone.
This two-way calling of the brain's prayer, Amen.
This park at night and also yellow lights.
This scary.
This sound of someone on fire and also how the body is all water.
This epilepsy and also the ground opening up and the ground closing.

SIDEWALK

My mother worked like a dog

for so long

it's nice to see her

be the owner—

There are only, really, one million

two hundred and ten ways

to die.

But my favorites are

your father drinking,

your father breathing,

your father

touching anything at all,

your father

listening to opera, your father

looking at you

and saying I see you. Like Pope Francis

looking at a girl's knees

when he was twelve and what made him love

Jesus lit up

right as she crossed her legs

in the sign of the cross.

Actually there are only ten ways

to die but I'm too afraid to say.

I'm brave enough

to walk home, though.

Brave enough for the dark

if there's a cross in it, a telephone pole,

or a weirdly shaped tree,

if there's a dog being walked,

if there's a dog at all.

In years to come, when you sign

all your letters

with your mind only, know

that someone is alone

in their bed with a body sort of like the body

you have and that she believes

that she is dying. That she is thinking about

her porous mother

and Scotch-taped father.

You go anywhere in the world,

even inside your own self,

and your mom and dad

will be right there

like two warm eggs

with a little chocolate and blood

inside them. I'm sorry

I was just thinking

about my mom and thinking about my dad

and thinking

about the blue plastic bags

people use to pick up after their dog,

because they love that stupid dog

so much, even though it's not a baby

and even though they can't have sex with it,

not really, not the way

you and I have sex,

with a ball and a stick, calling each other

in from the dark,

whispering good boy and whispering

good girl.

FOUR P.M.

I wonder about my brain and how it's a freeway and also tulips.
I wonder about your post-structuralism.
I wonder about your feet.
I wonder about the time I was twelve and also electrocution.
I wonder about the faces on milk cartons, 1981.
I wonder about what I've done.
I wonder about tunnels and bridges and both of them in the sky.
I wonder about my mother and father.
I wonder about the oxygen around your mouth.
I wonder about trees and lampposts and synergy and oxycodone and you.
I wonder about the hierarchy of Mass.
I wonder about the sounds you make and also pillowcases and coffee.
I wonder about what I'll do.
I wonder about what I didn't do and then it was two months.
I wonder about the yellow eyes of eggs and how you are not a currency.
I wonder about Justin and how the war is going.
I wonder about his body being torn apart.
I wonder about the nightmare of my body and the still pool of your lap.
I wonder about your fingers.
I wonder about paper bags and clouds and also it's September.
I wonder about hospital lighting.
I wonder about cancer and ginger ale and SWAT teams and their minds.
I wonder about the moon as an optician.
I wonder about how time bends and if I can bend it and also you.

SAINT FRANCIS AND THE PINE TREE

Before they beat me I knelt down
beneath the pine tree

and lowered
my head and placed my hands

in front of me like two plates,
together but lightly

so they wouldn't break, just like this,
like how a child's psychologist would do

with two dolls, one female
and one male, and ask

was it like this? My hands barely touching
so that you could draw a piece of floss

between them, and inside
the ten-year-old cave

I had made of myself, I thought
of Saint Francis and how he forgave

everyone and was poor
like me though he could have been rich,

and how he was always standing
beneath a tree or standing

with an animal that lived in trees,
and how he was kept alive by love,

and that was what I was going to do,
I knelt there

and smelled the pine
and said aloud

some made-up prayer
about forgiveness and that's

when the front of a skateboard
slammed into my face, into it

but also sort of through
my face, like a breeze

made out of wood and metal.
I looked up. I looked up into

the arms and stiff green needles
of the pine tree

and it seemed like a father
looking down on me the way fathers do

though the arms moved like a mother,
and I wasn't alone,

I had the boys who were beating me
for one, and the pine for the other.

After that I felt like every tree
knew who I was.

That I loved love, though
I had no real idea about it

or what to do. I mean
really what to do.

And then one of the boys held my arms
while another boy held my legs

while another boy pulled down my pants
while another boy grabbed a branch,

grabbed a part
of the pine tree that had fallen,

and waved it in front of my face and said
we're gonna stick it in you, we're gonna stick it

up your ass, but was a coward, or he was
also afraid and so just hit me with it

and laughed and then some wind came
because it doesn't care about shame or kids

and rose up beneath the pine
and with it some of the boys' brown hair

and the pine tree moved,
and the boys looked off at something else and then

followed after it, whatever unlucky thing
it was, and I sat there alone again

but for the pine and the light in the tree and the wind
and I thought of Saint Francis

and how he might stand up now and hug the tree
and call him brother for had not the tree

stood there and witnessed him, his body,
and so I stood up

in my rugged robe of blue jeans and T-shirt,
and hugged the tree, and kissed it, and thanked it

for not leaving me, and called it brother,
and then never came near it again,

for the following summer I felt God walk away
and chose my cock over sainthood,

and stood beneath a weeping willow and kissed
Angela Marquez and took her tongue

into my mouth and she took my fingers
into her body

and the willow moved above
and all around us,

it held us and kept us
until we were

done with one another
and then it let us go.

FIVE P.M.

I heard the dog crying all night in the car and felt right at home.
I heard the rain.
I heard about what was happening in that place.
I heard the freeway and elevators and landing gears and also nothing.
I heard I was dying.
I heard the room when the room walked away.
I heard the floor when I fainted.
I heard everything that was left over and also someone calling out.
I heard the brain seize up.
I heard about what happened and how it sounded really bad and I'm sorry.
I heard the call to prayer.
I heard white linen and floss and dispatches and a single piece of paper.
I heard dark all around.
I heard dark all around and a seashell.
I heard you would never come back and also the moon.
I heard the moon knocking its teeth out.
I heard the computer start up and the rice cooking and the groom smoking.
I heard myself and wanted to cut it into ribbons.
I heard the party start.
I heard people laughing at me and why shouldn't they?
I heard I hesitated.
I heard the expression on your face and people speaking in a submarine.
I heard the men in the stairwell.
I heard the biting and pulling and curled-up shaking in the bedroom.

BLACK FLAG

A nest not all the way at the top of the evergreen but almost,

rooted in between two branches

like a tooth,

a paper bag.

It's winter so inside

no one is home, no warm bodies ticking like feathery clocks,

just the wind in there, just whatever

you might imagine, but it's beautiful

up there and when I look at it it doesn't matter

what I've become because the nest is all clear even while it falls

apart, even as it melts

in the acid rain.

Who looks at something empty and doesn't think about what

they could fill it with? No one.

A needle, a body.

A nest.

A needle slipping in between your fingers, in between your toes.

WALKING THE DOGS

I haven't done drugs for three days so I name each one after
my sister and mother and brother and take them
out with me on a walk, each one taking turns leading, each one the leader
of a pack that was bred in the mid-
seventies,
each leash the color
of glass and the density of a star, I hold each
leash like something

that has returned home after being lost, I walk them under the oaks
and maples, under the lilacs and cherries, they walk
through the shadows like the team
they are, each
caring for the other
like I always wanted them to, each giving room for a paw, a tail,
sometimes smelling each other
to make sure they are alright, we are

all alright, the thing that is not God whispers to me, you are
not alone, you are not
a shovel or
a horse, even the stem
of the rosemary bush is really excited that you have made it this far, see
how it shivers

in the early spring breeze, see how it's a breeze to be with your

whole family,

to be the porch

they all sit on after dinner, mugs in their hands and wine in the mugs, and how

they lift their noses into the wind

and sniff and look to see

if you are there, if you are going to do

what you promised

to do, if you are going

to live and call them sometimes and tell them you love them.

SIX P.M.

This planet that's in outer space.
This way I am with strangers and silverware.
This exact time and trees.
This looking past your right ear and at the ocean.
This piece of limestone.
This grave I made out of dinner and a bottle of wine.
This bell ringing.
This hammer the size of my closet with me inside it.
This letter I wrote to you with the packet of honey inside it.
This razor with my family history inside it.
This room right now and how it's outside of everything.
This tired.
This talking and talking and wind and grass and midnight.
This ambulance in my hands.
This is how happy I am with you.
This thumb and mouth and ribbon and ice and asshole.
This Sunday.
This body like any other prescription-filled blue pill.
This weekend.
This ghost in your room pretending to be your older brother.
This pair of running shoes.
This afternoon.
This car that I'm driving made out of blood and guts and coupons.
This place like any other place.

CIRCLE JERKS

The starlings move

in one body made of many like the neighborhood, like

a hive gone mad. They move

like blood inside the hands of Holy Rollers, Christ-static

smothering

the church air.

A bunch of seeds in the air with wings.

A kind of all-or-nothing

silence

when they go to sleep in the chimneys. The baby starlings

underneath the mom and dad starlings.

Walking around here

I remember there was more than just what I remember,

more than garbage. There were animals in the sky

that moved like science fiction,

there were trees,

plants. There were dogs and cats

and a friend shooting up in your parents' bathroom

like a starling, suddenly, into the air and then gone again.

WONDERLAND

Caleb is doing it himself.
I have to do this myself,

he said. So I steal some beer from my mom
and he brings a sewing needle,

a towel, some ink. He's sitting
on his skateboard, dipping the needle

into the ink and then into his own skin,
over and over,

like an old lady working
on a country scene with thread.

This went on for a long time.
Then the thing began

to take shape, the lines became visible,
and soon it was all coming

together, the head first
and then the body of

the swastika

and finally it was whole and in the world.

Caleb's face flush

and sweaty and excited.

When he asked how it looked

I said it looked

good. I couldn't stop

looking at it

but when I looked up at him

it was like his face wasn't there.

EIGHT P.M.

I could blow my brains out and then I'd really get it.
I could walk all over this place and never remember who I am.
I could taxidermy and lunges.
I could lungs and blood vessels and cartilage and lift with my knees.
I could walk away.
I could hello everyone I'm so glad you're still here.
I could do lost keys and lost credit card and lost sock and also September.
I could in any room in your house.
I could light the light.
I could make it rain the way I am with you and also the freeway at night.
I could be here forever.
I could do the dying and let you do the funeral stuff, the sad stuff and all.
I could toy trains and mothballs and skeletons.
I could suck my thumb.
I could suck my thumb if you wanted me to.
I could do dusk and what is left moving around the leaves in the maples.
I could decide against it all and also my testicles.
I could run to the store and milk and baby please come back to bed.
I could beg the way I was taught to I am so good at it.
I could video games and hours of television and rosemary and cocaine.
I could make soup.
I could make tea and make it all up and also are you coming or going.
I could if I wanted to.
I could have been someone who lived.

GRASS MOON

My whole body is warm and sticky
like a child's car seat
just waiting, just waiting,
in the dark
the blue heron that lives
in Laurelhurst Park is breathing
and there is a wind
that is coming all over the flowers
and all the ferns. I'm on my way
to myself, that's what I'm told, that's what
all the people who want me
to be alive keep saying,
they keep standing on the beach
wearing old-fashioned swim trunks
with a bullhorn telling me about it,
and you are home in your bed
like a soft animal with really intense
feelers and a kind of knowledge
some people have to go out
into the desert to get,
some people have to take drugs for that
and walk barefoot over coals
and pretend that nature is a mother

always wringing her hands
over her lost children.
I'm making a museum for myself
out of pictures of people
I used to know and hold and their brains
are like carnations floating in milk
when I think of them I think
what do I really want
out of this branch I picked up off the street
which does not belong to me at all.
Last night I asked the ceiling
what was going to happen,
and it said this is what
is going to happen: you will have to
stay in your body for much longer
than you really want to,
and I thought about how nice it felt
the first time I shaved my head
and walked out into the rain
and how the rain walked
all over my head
and how when I hear someone yelling
something at someone else,

when I hear someone throwing

something across a room,

I want the world to be my laundry—

quiet and good and neatly folded away.

BLACK LIPSTICK

My little sister is sneaking her friends out the back door of a bar
  because the men in there won't stop touching them

and the people in the bar
  won't stop the men and the men keep ordering sweet

drinks they think the women will like but they don't want them.
  All they want to do is leave and live.

When I get out of the shower and look in the mirror I say to myself
  you should go to the gym, you should lose weight, be more

handsome. People who rape
  other people have bodies like mine, people who hate their wives

and daughters. They hate them and go to the bar
  and drink too much and touch people who do not want to be touched.

I don't know.
  I miss being young and going out in eyeliner and skirts. I miss

wearing black lipstick. Fucking boys

    and girls was the best. It felt like drinking iced Americanos

on the roof of the roof of the world. From there you were safe, you could

    smoke clove cigarettes with your friends.

You could throw rocks at the men down below, walking down the street

    with their brains in one hand and their hearts in another,

a parade of terrible potential, while their mothers stand along the sidewalk

    clapping and cheering, waving

baby-blue handkerchiefs in the cold air.

WONDERLAND

Caleb is marching
with his new friends, their shaved heads

like tongues of fire,
up 82nd Avenue, the cars honking at them

like they were vets
just home from the war. He must feel

so safe in his skin.
He must feel like he belongs.

With each step, each time
he raises his arm in the air

at that angle we all know,
a part of him

transforms, a part of him
fades and in its place is something more

vulnerable than a worm.
He is swinging

a metal pipe in a hand
that looks like an insect's pincer,

his face looks like a piece
of fruit covered in flies.

Every time he takes a step
his childhood evaporates,

branches begin to crawl
out of his head, rise up like antlers.

MIDNIGHT

Now everything is going to be antidepressants and roses.
Now I get to go home for real.
Now the light in the bathroom is flickering.
Now my brain is jump ropes and licorice and also tubes.
Now my mother is calling.
Now my father is coming home.
Now fluorescent lights and the unbuttoning inside the MRI.
Now don't look at me.
Now let's just all calm down and what exactly happened here.
Now tissue paper and magazines.
Now I can just hide in bed and carve our initials into the bark.
Now moonlight and lip balm.
Now say whatever it is you were going to say.
Now settlements and rocket launchers and also I have champagne.
Now I can be the air I have always wanted to be.
Now you won't be bothered.
Now the doors and the windows and the fuzzy-peach streetlight.
Now don't touch me.
Now don't worry there's enough here for everyone I promise.
Now parades and confetti and sugar-covered almonds.
Now the extraterrestrial abandonment of the self.
Now razors and bathtubs and fifty milligrams of Valium.
Now this is happening of course it is.
Now this is not what I expected I'm sorry it will only take a minute.

BIG LOVE

All weekend my friend Jacob has been trying to land a 360 No Comply, he spends
hours skating at the mall and in Chinatown where he's been experimenting with
pills he crushes up
and then inhales.
High school
is out there
somewhere
waiting for us.

All weekend he has been talking me out of my sadness. You have to disappear into it.
At Jacob's house we pick up two cans of generic root beer and tighten the trucks on
his board.
His mother is
sitting on a
stool in the middle
of the living room,
half naked,

half covered in a robe. It's summer and the can of root beer feels like a lake
in my hand. As we walk toward the front door Jacob's mom is laughing. What
are you two faggots
doing anyway,
she says, you

guys gonna

fuck each other?

And then

there's a weird silence and then Jacob punches her in the face, off the stool
and onto the floor. This is the mother and son disappearing. Like an old
television screen,

all static,

then dark,

then who

knows what

after that.

ACKNOWLEDGMENTS

Grateful acknowledgment is made to the editors of the following publications in which some of these poems have appeared in earlier drafts:

American Poetry Review, *The Believer*, *The Boston Review*, *Hunger Mountain*, *The New Yorker*, *The Well Review* (Ireland), and *Zyzzyva*.

All the "hour" poems first appeared as a chapbook titled *24 Hours*. This chapbook was first printed in Paris, France, in 2014, by Onestar Press and then in the United States later that same year by Poor Claudia.

Both "White Power" and "For Ian Sullivan Upon Joining the Eastside White Pride" first appeared in a chapbook titled *Something About a Black Scarf* published by Azul Editions in 2008.

I am also grateful for the sustaining support of both the Guggenheim and Civitella Ranieri Foundations, without which a lot of these poems wouldn't have been written.

I am honored to have had the support of amazing friends including Carl Adamshick, Kazim Ali, Elizabeth Austin, Samiya Bashir, Sean Aaron Bowers, Ernie Casciato, Trinie Dalton, Jason Dodge, Carolyn Forché, Jessica Grindell, Major Jackson, Thomas Lauderdale, Dorianne Laux, Matthew Lippman, Michael McGriff, Joseph Millar, Jay Nebel, D. A. Powell, Geoff Rickly, Christine Roland, Mary Ruefle, Ed Skoog, Mark Waldron, Ahren Warner, C. K. Williams, Kevin Young, The Greater Trumps.

Thanks to the wonderful Bill Clegg.

Deep gratitude is owed to Jill Bialosky for her continued faith, insight, and care.

Thank you to Drew Elizabeth Weitman for her patience and guidance.

This book would not be what it is without the suggestions and big vision of my brother Michael Dickman.

It would have been impossible to have completed this book without the love, help, critical eye, and life shared with Julia Tillinghast.

Love and honor to my little sister Elizabeth Dickman.

Thanks to all the different formations of my family: from the Dickmans to Tillinghasts to Vanhandles to Huddlestons to Castelluccis to Nobles.

And with special praise to my mother, Wendy Dickman.